G000094936

The Abundance Zone

Steve Oxlade and Matt Traverso

Please visit

www.TheAbundanceZone.com

Cover and Book Design
by Neil Coe (neil@cartadesign.co.uk)

Set in 'The Serif' 10pt on 13.5pt

First published in 2007 by;

Ecademy Press

6 Woodland Rise, Penryn,
Cornwall UK TR10 8QD
info@ecademy-press.com
www.ecademy-press.com

Printed and Bound by;
Lightning Source in the UK and USA

Printed on acid-free paper from managed forests. This book is
printed on demand, so no copies will be remaindered or pulped.

ISBN 978-1-905823-21-5

A CIP catalogue record for this title is available from the British
Library

Acknowledgements

We would like to thank all those who have inspired us to write this book.

Particular thanks go to Judy May Murphy, Gerry Robert and Mindy Gibbins-Klein (and her team at ecademy Press) who all guided us through the publishing maze, to Neil Coe of Carta Design for the excellent design work, and to Caroline Newman for being such a loving soul and helping to make this book happen.

And most of all we want to thank you, the reader, for getting ready to embark upon a transformational journey which will propel you towards the life that you truly desire.

*It is one of the most beautiful compensations
of this life that no man can sincerely try to
help another without helping himself....
Serve and thou shall be served*

Ralph Waldo Emerson

Contents

"You wanted and deserved abundance. Now read and absorb my friend Steve's book and utilize its wisdom to make abundance yours permanently!"

Mark Victor Hansen
Best selling co-author of the *Chicken Soup for the Soul* series and *One Minute Millionaire*

"A powerful yet simple guide to transforming your life through the power of words."

Gerry Robert
**Best selling author of *The Millionaire Mindset*
www.gerryrobert.com**

"This jewel will help ignite your passion for life in exchange for just a few moments each day!"

Mike Dooley
**Author of *Notes from the Universe* and star of *The Secret* movie
www.tut.com**

Foreword

In life we are blessed with amazing experiences where we are effortlessly reminded of the abundance in our lives, no matter how many seminars or courses we attend there will be times we are presented with 'tests' where we may question the resources we have available to us. *The Abundance Zone* provides us with the **conditioning** to focus on and attract even more abundance in any area of our lives minimising the moments of lack that may present to us.

Abundance is a mind set, a way of being, this book and the resources that Steve Oxlade and Matt Traverso are attracting into *The Abundance Zone* definitely inspire us all to become even more resourceful.

Use this book as an additional tool in your toolbox of resources to support you, and those you love, to live a life of abundance. Commit to actively participating in the questions and prompts ensuring that this tool is sharp, charged and ready for action in your life, as and when you need it.

Steve are Matt are individuals who live in *The Abundance Zone*. Having known Steve for many years, he embodies abundance in core areas of life - Health, Wealth, Relationship, Emotions, Spirituality and Contribution.

As with all abundance comes from an awareness of gratitude, I would like to thank Steve and Matt for all their contribution to so many individuals and organisations they have inspired and are yet to.

I wish you all a life of abundance where you witness the cycle where being even more grateful brings you even more to be grateful for.

Harry Singha
Chair, YES Group London
Chair and Co-founder, Youth Coaching Academy
Social Entrepreneur

"A simple, practical book that everyone can read to improve the quality of their life."

Paul McKenna

the world's leading hypnotist and Europe's most successful personal development author

"Steve Oxlade and Matt Traverso have produced a phenomenal resource for us all to fill up our minds with the words that the most successful and abundant people on the planet habitually use. What I love about this book is that at any moment in your day you can just open it and allow yourself to be reminded and inspired of certain words which will trigger deep inside of you certain feelings or flashes of awareness that will propel you forward in the direction of your destiny."

Dave O'Connor

**Co-Founder of the Effortless Living Institute, Author, *NLP Master Practitioner* and leading authority on personal power and effectiveness
www.DaveOConnor.info**

Introduction

Do you know what abundant and successful people have in common?

They have mastered their language, both internally and externally. They use the words and language of abundance: the A-Z of Successful Living. They are living in *The Abundance Zone*!

We would like to share with you the words and language that successful people habitually use in their lives. The words and language you actually use CAN and WILL have a profound effect on your emotional and physical life.

For example the words *I can't* can be limiting and set boundaries to what you may want to achieve, and the words as simple as *I can*, will empower your mind and heart, unleashing your imagination and giving you access to the unlimited possibilities of how you can achieve whatever you want!

Recent research has shown that words have a powerful impact on our emotional state and wellbeing. Positive words have a higher vibrational energy. Some words will challenge you to step out of your comfort zones and experience new adventurous ways of living and others will even set you free.

In our experience the more we habitually used these words in our daily lives, the more our lives accelerated towards our goals and dreams, with more passion and fulfilment than ever before.

We invite you in this book to share with us the positive experience of empowering words – words that inspire and actively create your experience of life moment to moment – words that shape your destiny.

And remember, this book is called *The Abundance Zone* because it is not only applicable to wealth but to health, relationships and wherever you want to experience true abundance.

Welcome to *The Abundance Zone*.

Steve Oxlade and Matt Traverso

Favourite Quotes

The moment one definitely commits oneself then Providence moves too. All sorts of things occur to help one that would never otherwise have occurred.... unforeseen incidents, meeting, and material assistance, which no man could have dreamed would have come his way.
— *Johann Wolfgang von Goethe*

When you realise that nothing is lacking, the whole world belongs to you. — *Lao Tzu*

Those who have failed to work toward the truth have missed the purpose of living. — *Buddha*

Your sole business in life is to attain God-realisation. All else is useless and worthless.
— *Sivananda*

Should we all confess our sins to one another we would laugh at once for our lack of originality.
— *Gibran*

Dance as though no one is watching you,

Love as though you have never been hurt before,

Sing as though no one can hear you,

Live as though heaven is on earth. — *Souza*

The Abundance Zone

Your A-Z of Successful Living

We have selected for your benefit, the most empowering words we could find from A to Z, from Abundance to Zone.

At the same time, we have deliberately kept this guide light and concise, so that you can take its wisdom with you whenever you need inspiration.

To further enjoy the many benefits of this book, we would highly recommend that you take a few moments to answer for yourself the questions on the right hand side of each word.

This will really enhance your experience with this material and it allows you the personal time and space to start creating your destiny.

Get ready to...

Make your life a masterpiece!

is for...

Abundance	Having more than you need in all aspects of your life, including wealth, health, happiness and relationships.
Achievement	It is not what you achieve but how many others you help along the way.
Action	The greatest idea is useless without action. Massive action is what launches your journey towards the stars.
Affluence	An affluent mind creates affluence in your life.
Ambition	Those with the smallest ambitions usually work for those with the largest.
Appreciation	Life without appreciation is like trying to drive a car without fuel or crossing the desert without water.
Attention	Pay attention to your thoughts – as they manifest. Pay positive attention.
Attitude	Attitude is a small thing, which can make a huge difference. Your Attitude determines your Altitude in life.

Your Daily Questions: **Your Answers:** (please enter these now!)

Your Daily Questions	Your Answers
How can you remove lack from your life and cultivate an **abundance** mentality?	
What would you want to **achieve**, if you knew you could not fail?	
What massive **action** can you take right now to catapult yourself closer to your destiny?	
How can you attract more **affluence** right now?	
What **ambitions** could take you to another level?	
What 3 things in your life could you **appreciate** more?	
How can you pay **attention** to what you want to achieve and manifest?	
What **attitudes** can you decide to change right now to make the biggest difference in your life?	

is for...

Balance	Balance will allow you to dance through life, rather than stumble.
Beauty	Life is full of beauty. Look around you and savour it at every moment.
Being	Remember that you are a human being, not a human doing.
Belief	Whatever you believe will be true for you. If you believe you can do something, then you are right. If you believe that you cannot, then you are also right.
Breathe	When you breathe properly, you give your body the gift of Oxygen and Life.
Best	Go first class all the way, and the universe will provide you with the best.
Bliss	If bliss is an option, then why would you choose anything else?

Your Daily Questions:	**Your Answers:** (please enter these now!)
What can bring more **balance** to your life?	
How many **beautiful** things can you see, hear and feel around you right now?	
How can you be more by doing less?	
What is one **belief** that does not serve you? How much is it costing you? How much more will it cost you if you continue for another year? What about 3, 5, 10 years? Now, when will you change your **belief**?	
How much energy can you generate with three deep **breaths** right now?	
How can you expand your comfort zone by opting for the **best**?	
How can you cultivate a state of **bliss** right now?	

Certainty	A fundamental human need. The most successful people can comfortably handle the most uncertainty.
Choices	Life is about choices, choose wisely.
Change	The river of life flows and turns in many directions. Learn to swim with the tide as well.
Compassion	Practice compassion, it's humbling and allows your heart to connect.
Confidence	Inner confidence - the ability to really trust yourself - is already within you. Own it!
Connection	Connection is vital in experiencing all around you, universe and source. It's what makes us special.
Contribution / Charity	What you give returns to you tenfold, it's a law of the universe.
Conviction	When a belief becomes strong enough it becomes a conviction.
Courage	Courage is when you go ahead despite feeling afraid.
Creativity	Everyone has the capacity to be creative. Some just don't know it yet.

Your Daily Questions: **Your Answers:** (please enter these now!)

Your Daily Questions	Your Answers
How can you create more **certainty** about something important to you?	
How can I be thankful for the **choices** I have in life?	
What can you **change** today to take you to the next level?	
What situation in your life can you be more **compassionate** about?	
When was the last time you felt really **confident** and how can you use this experience every time?	
Connect to someone next to you, smile and notice how it makes you feel.	
How can you **contribute** right now?	
What positive belief could you strengthen to become a **conviction**?	
What fears can you push aside to challenge yourself to practice your **courage**?	
How can you let your own **creativity** shine through?	

is for...

Dance	Dance allows you the freedom of expression of body and spirit. It is a great, fun exercise and stress reliever as well.
Decision	Your destiny is shaped in your moments of decision. Leaders make decisions quickly and change them slowly.
Design	We all have the ability to design our own life, as we want it.
Desire	Those who have a burning desire, will get to their goals the fastest.
Destiny	We all have a destiny, and the quicker we identify it, the more strongly we will flow towards it.
Determination	When all else fails, determination will get you there.
Direction	You may take many paths, as long as you keep heading in the direction of your destiny. It is like a compass that guides you through life.
Divine	If you choose to follow the divine, you will never feel alone.

Your Daily Questions: **Your Answers:** (please enter these now!)

Your Daily Questions	Your Answers
In how many fun ways can you move your body right now for the next 30 seconds?	
What **decisions** have you been putting off until now, and how freeing does it feel to have made the decision?	
How can you make your life a masterpiece?	
What do you really **desire** with a burning passion?	
If you knew what your **destiny** was, what would it be?	
Where could more **determination** help you in your life?	
Are all the things planned for today helping you to head in the right **direction**?	
What **divine** guidance would help you right now?	

is for...

Effortless	Life can be effortless if you choose it to be. This is when you go with the flow, rather than battle against it.
Emotion	Emotions are a key driving force and can be either your servants or destroyers. Fortunately, you can decide which, because you have the ability to change state in a heart-beat.
Energy	Energy is everywhere.
Excellence	If excellence is an option, why settle for any less?
Exercise	Exercise is the basis to form habits, and habits shape your life.
Expectation	Expect only the best in life, but remove your attachment to the outcome and you will never be disappointed if it has not happened yet for you.

Your Daily Questions: **Your Answers:** (please enter these now!)

Your Daily Questions	Your Answers
How much less stressful would your life be, if you decided to follow the **effortless** route?	
How can you use your **emotions** in a positive way to propel you forward?	
Close your eyes and notice the **energy** all around you.	
Where can you show **excellence** in your life today?	
What can you **exercise** and practice to really master an important area of your life?	
What great **expectations** do you have of your life?	

is for...

Faith	Have faith in yourself and the universe always if you want to lead a more fulfilling life.
Feedback	There is no failure in life, only feedback. If at first you don't succeed, then change your approach.
Flow	Life becomes effortless when you take advantage of the natural flow of life and move with it in perfect harmony.
Focus	Focus will help you hit your bullseye more often than missing the target completely.
Freedom	Enjoy the freedom you have in life.
Friendship	Even strangers are friends who we have not met yet.
Fulfillment	Ultimately, we all want to feel fulfilled in life. Few people know that fulfillment comes from within.
Fun	Without fun, life is meaningless.

Your Daily Questions: **Your Answers:** (please enter these now!)

Your Daily Questions	Your Answers
*How can you have more **faith** in yourself and the universe?*	
What can you learn from your last "disaster"?	
*Would you rather **flow** with the river of life, or struggle against the tide?*	
*How can you **focus** more to ensure that you remain on track?*	
*What has to happen for you to feel even more **free** in your life?*	
*Who can you make a **friend** today?*	
*How quickly can you decide to feel **fulfilled** at any point during the day?*	
*How can you have more **fun** with your work, relationships and life?*	

Giving / Generosity	The more you sow the more you reap. This is an immutable law of life, and usually the return is ten-fold.
Goal	How can you get from A to B without knowing where B is? Aim for your target and make it huge and clear, because you will find it much easier to hit.
God	The Universe, Divine, Lord, Life – it does not matter what you call it, as long as you realize that there is a Higher Power which has your best intentions in mind, if only you have the faith which will allow you to notice it.
Gratitude	Be grateful for all the little things in life, which combine to ultimately make a big difference, and be grateful for what you have in life, don't regret the things you don't have.
Growth	A fundamental human need is to learn and grow.
Guide	Let Life guide you by going with the flow.

Your Daily Questions: Your Answers: (please enter these now!)

Your Daily Questions	Your Answers
What can you **give** today, because you never know when you may need some help in the future?	
What do you want and when do you want it?	
When was the last time you felt guided?	
What 3 things can you be **grateful** for in your life right now?	
What can you do today to **grow** to the next level?	
How can you go with the flow today?	

is for...

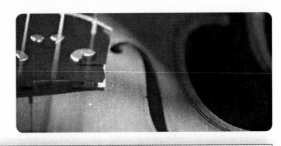

Habit	Our habits form our lifestyle.
Happiness	Ultimately, what people want from life beyond money and material goods is happiness.
Harmony	Harmony leads to a blissful life where everything flows smoothly.
Health	Health is the single most important area throughout your life, because what good are millions in wealth when you feel too unwell to enjoy them?
Heart	Life moves to a new level when you stop thinking with your head and start listening with your heart.
Higher Power	God, Life, the Universe – whatever you want to call it, it is there when you need it.
Hilarity	Hilarity and laughter make the world run smoother.
Honesty	Before being honest to others, you need to be honest to yourself.

Your Daily Questions:	**Your Answers:** (please enter these now!)
What good **habits** can you start acquiring today?	
How can you decide to be **happy** right now, and whenever you want?	
What can you do today to create more **harmony** in your life and those around you?	
What can you do today to move towards the **healthy** lifestyle that you desire?	
How can you listen more with your **heart** today?	
How can you tap into this **Higher Power** now?	
In what can you find **hilarity** today?	
What has being dis**honest** cost you in your life and in your relationships?	

Idea	Ideas are great when you get them, but worthless unless you use them.
Ideal	In a universe of perfection, everything is ideal.
Identity	Probably the most powerful driving force is to align with your identity, so make yours one which you can be proud of.
Infinite	Imagine a universe with infinite space; now imagine a universe with infinite possibilities.
Inspiration	Push others and you will struggle against the smallest boulders. Inspire others and you can move the largest mountains.
Integrity	Integrity is doing the right thing, even when nobody else is watching.
Intention	Often it is not so much the action taken, but the intention behind it, which determines a successful outcome.

Your Daily Questions: **Your Answers:** (please enter these now!)

Your Daily Questions	Your Answers
What great **ideas** have you still not yet implemented?	
How can you see the **ideal** in yourself, others and things around you?	
Who are you, really?	
How can you incorporate the concept of **infinite** positive possibilities to your day today?	
How can you **inspire** those around you today?	
How does it feel to live with **integrity**?	
What **intentions** guide your actions? Are these true to your purpose?	

J is for...

Jedi Knight	It is not a matter whether you can, but whether you awaken to what you are truly capable of.
Jewel	People search the seven seas and climb the highest mountains to find those elusive jewels, yet they often forget to look in the one place untouched: inside them.
Join	Find something you like, and join forces, so that you can share the joys and spoils ahead.
Journey	If life is a journey, then choose your vehicles wisely.
Joy	If joy and happiness are an option, then why settle for anything less?

Your Daily Questions: **Your Answers:** (please enter these now!)

Your Daily Questions	Your Answers
What could you achieve if you realized that you already have all the power that you need, right now?	
*Where are the **jewels** in your life?*	
*Who or what can you **join** today?*	
*Which vehicle(s) will give you the best ride on your **journey** through life?*	
*How can you create more **joy** for yourself and those around you?*	

Karma	Karma is the law of return. Treat people and the universe around you with loving intention. Only love will fill your life in return.
Key	A key distinction is a little thing, which can unlock a vast treasure.
Kindness	Kindness is about being gentle and being human. Start by being kind to yourself.
Knowledge	Information is powerless until it is structured into knowledge.

Your Daily Questions: **Your Answers:** (please enter these now!)

Your Daily Questions	Your Answers
How can you be more loving to people around you? How can you be more loving to the universe?	
What is **key** in your life?	
How many acts of **kindness** can you extend today?	
What **knowledge** can you use today?	

L is for...

Language	The language we use with ourselves and others is impactful. Choose the words you speak carefully.
Laugh	If you can laugh at an unpleasant event when looking back at it, then why wait when you can laugh at that time?
Learning	Never stop learning, because when you stop growing, you die.
Letting Go	Letting Go of old memories and behaviours frees up space for new experiences and relationships.
Light	The light inside you shines much brighter than any other light that you seek during your darkest hours.
Life	Life is a gift, so embrace it and make the most of it.
Love	Love is the only freedom in the world because it so elevates the spirit that the laws of humanity and the phenomena of nature do not alter its course – K Gibran
Luxury	Treat yourself to the best in life, and life will treat you to the best.

Your Daily Questions:	**Your Answers:** (please enter these now!)
How can you use more positive inspiring **language** daily?	
How can you incorporate more **laughter** into your life?	
What new things can you **learn** today, and how can you apply them in your life?	
What can you **let go** of that no longer serves you or your identity?	
How can you shine your **light** to help others today?	
In what ways can you embrace **life** even more?	
How can you fill your life with more **love**?	
What can you treat yourself to today?	

is for... M

Magic Moments	Life is not measured by the number of breaths we take, but by the moments that take our breath away.
Making Love	Enjoy the loving exchange of making love. It is the magic of the miraculous creation of new life.
Manifest	Every manifestation starts with a thought, so make sure that you choose your thoughts wisely.
Masterpiece	Make your life a masterpiece.
Mastery	If you want to learn something new, why stop short of mastery?
Meditation	Be still and witness life in its full glory!
Message/ Messenger	Learn to separate the message from the messenger.
Money	Money is a method of exchange of products and services. Those with the most money are those who have given the most or provided the most service.
Motivation	Ask not who can motivate you, but who you can motivate.
Music	Music is the voice of the soul, and the rhythm of life.

Your Daily Questions: **Your Answers:** (please enter these now!)

Your Daily Questions	Your Answers
What **magic moments** can you remember from this week, and what others can you create today?	
How can you experience spirit when **making love**? In what ways can you give thanks for this magical union?	
What have you **manifest**ed into your life in the past, and what would you like to manifest next?	
What **masterful** strokes can you contribute today?	
What can I learn and **master** today?	
When will you schedule your daily **meditations**?	
What **messages** can you learn from today?	
What is your relationship with **money**, and does it serve you?	
Who can you **motivate** right now?	
How can you incorporate more **music** into your life?	

is for... **N**

Nature	Nature yields her most profound secrets to the person who has powerful reasons to uncover them.
New	It is only through a new focus, a new decision, a new course of action that you can change your life. Never be afraid to try something new. Remember: amateurs built the ark, professionals built the Titanic!
Now	Now is the only time that exists and over which you have any control. Repeat the following incantation until the words become as much a habit as your breathing: "I will act now. This is the time. This is the place. I am the person." The past is history, the future is a mystery and 'now' is the most precious thing, that is why they call it the present.
Nurture	Nurture yourself, love yourself, and consciously savor the things you do for yourself. Until you can give love and nurture to yourself you cannot healthily give them to anyone else

Your Daily Questions: **Your Answers:** (please enter these now!)

What are your most compelling reasons to uncover life's greatest secrets?	
*What **new** things can you focus on – and act upon! – right now?*	
How can you find and appreciate - even more - the perfection of this moment?	
*What are some new playful ways you can **nurture** yourself today?*	

Oneness	Build for your team a feeling of oneness, of interdependence between one another. A successful team beats with one heart.
Opportunity	People wait for opportunity to come along... yet it is there every morning.
Options	Learn to see more options. Remember, if you only see one option, you have no options. If you see only two options then you have a dilemma. When you can see at least three options – now you are at choice and you can exercise freedom.
Outcome	Before starting with any plan or action, visualize clearly in your mind its successful outcome. If you visualize with concentration and faith, you will be amazed at the results.
Outstanding	Outstanding isn't a skill – It's a standard. It is HEART.

Your Daily Questions: **Your Answers:** (please enter these now!)

Questions	Answers
How can you use the miracle of **oneness** *as an unlimited source of power, love, and energy?*	
When would now be a good time to make use of **opportunity**? *That's not up to the opportunity. That's up to you.*	
How many **options** *do you have right now?* *(Enjoy your freedom as you think about the answers!)*	
How can you make sure your **outcome** *for today is in line with your ultimate outcome for your life?*	
What worthy goal will you give your heart and soul to?	

is for...

Passion	Nobody can be truly successful unless he's passionate about his work.
Peace	Peace starts with a smile.
Perfect	Life is already perfect. Just sometimes we tend to forget this, and allow negative emotions to cloud our vision of the perfection that has always been there.
Persistence	How long should you try? Until.
Positive	The first and most powerful change is to shift your mental focus from negative to positive.
Possibility	The only way to discover the limits of the possible is to go beyond them into the impossible.
Potentiality	No matter what you may have been led to believe, you have more potential than you can ever develop in a lifetime.
Power	If only we knew that we are powerful beyond measure.
Principle	Principles are those fundamentals of life that never change – things like integrity, faith, love and balance.
Purpose	Your life is God's gift to you...what you make of it is your gift back.

Your Daily Questions:	**Your Answers:** (please enter these now!)
What are you really **passionate** about?	
How would you smile, if right now you felt totally permeated by **peace**?	
How can you use your desire to be "**perfect**" to sculpt your greatness?	
How long will you try?	
What 10 **positive** things in your life can you think about right now?	
How can you use your imagination to attempt the "impossible"?	
What would you attempt to do if you knew you could not fail?	
How can you appreciate even more your unlimited **power**?	
What key organizing **principles** will you live by from now on?	
What's your **purpose**?	

Quality	Your focus on quality – rather than cutting costs – will make you a fortune. And in the long run, quality always costs less!
Quantum	A quantum success jump is analogous to shifting gears.
Quest	Joseph Campbell was right--the power of myth is that the great quest stories are really just parables about the journey within. The greatest quest is the internal one: the journey to your heart.
Questions	Questions are the answer!

Your Daily Questions: **Your Answers:** (please enter these now!)

Your Daily Questions	Your Answers
What's something you can improve upon and add value to in your life?	
What new gear can you shift to?	
*Where is your **quest** taking you? Is your greatest quest consistent with your values?*	
*What new **question(s)** can you ask yourself right now that will uplift your spirit and drive you along the path of human excellence?*	

is for...

Ready	Many people go to their grave with their song still in them. Why is this so? Too often it is because they are always getting ready to live. Before they know it, they run out of time. Don't let that be you.
Receiving	Value receiving. Allow someone else the gift of giving.
Relationship	Our relationships with others are essentially a reflection of our relationship with ourselves.
Reward	The greatest reward for doing is the opportunity to do more.
Rich	Getting rich starts with your thoughts. Think big, and you will become big!
Root	The roots of successful living lie in the will to become the best that you can become.

Your Daily Questions:	**Your Answers:** (please enter these now!)
What will you do today to demonstrate to yourself that you are as **ready** as you can be?	
How can I **receive** graciously today?	
How can you nurture and take better care of the **relationship** you have with yourself?	
How can you make the greatest and best use of the ever-expanding opportunity you have to do more?	
Who can you choose to mentor you to financial freedom?	
What are you committed to becoming?	

S is for ...

Service	Make service your first priority, not success and success will follow.
Simple	Simplicity is sustainability. Simplify!
Source	In order to change anything in your life, always see yourself as the source of the change, not the effect.
Spending	Trust me: It is by spending ourselves that we become rich!
Spirit	Spirit is the essence of being human. Connect with your spirit and feel your presence, because there is nothing more empowering than your personal connection with your soul.
State	State dictates. The state of your mind determines the state of your results.
Success	You are a smashing success when you are able to spend your life in your own way.

Your Daily Questions: **Your Answers:** (please enter these now!)

Your Daily Questions	Your Answers
*How can you better **serve** your customers and reach more people?*	
*How can you **simplify** a newly acquired skill in order to make it a habit?*	
When can you change? When will you change? Who's in charge now?	
*How can you **spend** yourself more completely?*	
How can you maximize your contribution that your life represents to the human spirit? *What is the essence of your **spirit**?*	
What would you do if you knew you could not fail?	
What can you do to show yourself that you are truly living the life you want?	

is for...

Tenacious	Those who complain about their lack of success simply haven't persevered and been tenacious.
Thought	We are what we think about most. With our thoughts we make our world.
Timeless	Key organizing principles are timeless – they never change.
Tithing	If you want great wealth and success in your life, begin the loving art of tithing today, by giving to those who need your love, inspiration and limitless power!
Total	Totally surrender to your Creator
Transcend	Transcend even the harshest conditions.
Truth	Telling yourself the truth – confiding with the self – is the basis of self-confidence.

Your Daily Questions: **Your Answers:** (please enter these now!)

Your Daily Questions	Your Answers
*What commitment can you make right now to strengthen your **tenacity**?*	
*How can you **think** and grow rich?*	
What are the principles you're going to live by from this day forward?	
*When would now be a good time to start **tithing**?*	
*What can you do **totally** today?*	
*What obstacle will you **transcend** today?*	
How can you be more honest with yourself today?	

Unbounded	Your internal power knows no bounds, except for the illusion in your mind, and the comfort zone formed by misguided habits.
Unconditional	Give unconditionally, and you will receive far more than you ever imagined.
Unconscious	The unconscious mind holds the vast untapped resources that will deliver your dreams, as soon as you are ready!
Understanding	Understanding what to do is not enough. It is only the first step. Action is the true way forward.
Unity / Unified	"We" are all one, there is only one.
Universe	The Universe is everything, then you have everything at your disposal whenever you simply ask.
Unlimited	Deep inside us we possess unlimited powers.
Uplifting	Every thought can be uplifting, if we only decide so.

Your Daily Questions: **Your Answers:** (please enter these now!)

Your Daily Questions	Your Answers
How can you step out of your comfort zone right now?	
*What gifts can you give **unconditionally** today?*	
*Are you ready to allow the **unconscious** to do its work for you?*	
*How fast can you start acting upon your **understandings**?*	
*How much simpler is the world when we accept our **unity**?*	
*What will you ask the **Universe** for first?*	
Are you ready to unleash your power within?	
*Who can you **lift up** and make their day?*	

Values	Values are the criteria against which you make decisions.
Victory	Every victory in life begins in your mind.
Vision	Vision is the outcome of all ultimate outcomes?
Vitality	Vitality is power. It's energy.
Vivacious	Vivacious people are truly alive, bursting with energy and leading a life full of fun and fulfillment.

Your Daily Questions: **Your Answers:** (please enter these now!)

Your Daily Questions	Your Answers
*What are your top 10 **values** in your life?*	
*What is your personal **victory** for today?*	
*Be sure to spend at least an hour every day focusing single-mindedly on your magnificent **vision**!*	
*What can you do to generate more **vitality** in everything that you do.*	
Are you truly alive? When would now be a good time to unleash your aliveness?	

is for…

Want	It doesn't matter how much you want. What matters is how much you want it.
Wealth	Happiness is a choice. Wealth is a decision.
Why	'Knowing why' is 80% of success. 'Knowing how' is only 20%.
Wisdom	Never mistake knowledge for wisdom. A loving heart is the truest wisdom.
World	The world is as you see it. It's your mind, not the world that is the source of all your experience.

Your Daily Questions: **Your Answers:** (please enter these now!)

*How much do you **want** it?*	
What new action can you take to back up your decision?	
***Why** do you want to be successful? What will it give you? **Why** is that important for you?*	
How can you appreciate and love the perfection of it all?	
*How can you now represent your **world** in a new empowering way?*	

eXpression	The only way to achieve true success is to express yourself completely, in your own unique way, in service to society.

Yearning	When you make your vision your true yearning, you will certainly achieve it and by all of God's universal laws you will always receive it!
Yes	Y. E. S.: Your Excellence Succeeds!
Yin and Yang	Yin and Yang: A blend of opposites for perfect harmony
Youthfulness	We do not stop playing because we grow old; we grow old because we stop playing. Never Be The First To Get Old!

Your Daily Questions: **Your Answers:** (please enter these now!)

How can you **express** and share more of who you are?	

Your Daily Questions: **Your Answers:** (please enter these now!)

What are you truly **yearning** for?	
What higher level of excellence can you commit to right now?	
How can you use this understanding to have more harmony in your life?	
How will you make your **youthfulness** everlasting?	

Z

is for...

Zeal	Experience shows that success is due less to ability than to zeal. Life cannot deny itself to the person who gives life his all.
Zen	The only Zen you find on the tops of mountains is the Zen you bring up there.
Zest	If we want to inspire our people to face the future with zest and self-confidence, we must educate them to be original as well as competent.
Zone	You are in the Zone when you are spending time on the things that matter most to you.

Your Daily Questions: **Your Answers:** (please enter these now!)

Your Daily Questions	Your Answers
What will you give your body and soul to?	
*How much **Zen** do you have?*	
*How can you exude more vitality, enthusiasm and **zest** for life?*	
What's most important to you in life, and how can you spend more time there every day?	

CONGRATULATIONS !!!

Integrating these into your Life

We trust that you have enjoyed reading and playing with these powerful words, and filled in your answers to your Daily Questions.

It's been a privilege to have shared these thoughts and ideas with you. We know that you're one of the few who do, versus the many who talk. Lots of people say they want to change their life but you've actually done something about it; so you have both our respect and appreciation for that. And we hope we'll have a chance to meet you some time in a seminar or some time in person.

Until we meet personally, remember that everything you strive to achieve comes from your ability to choose empowering words that truly define your experience.

In the meantime, for some more fun exercises, how about playing with the letters and forming more empowering words based on the letters which make up their essence. An example is shown below:

Attitude	-	Our attitude defines our level of abundance.
Belief	-	If we believe that we can do it then we are right, if we don't then we are also right.
Universe	-	Trust the Universe will provide whatever we desire.
Natural	-	Abundance is our Natural state.
Desire	-	The level of you desire will define the level of your success.
Action	-	Dreams manifest with action on your part.
Now	-	Be in the now, not in the past or the future.
Contribution	-	The more you give, the more you will receive.
Effortless	-	Follow the above and abundance will come effortlessly to you.

What other word(s) can you come up with each day?

Other Life Enhancing

Abundance Zone

Products

Abundance Zone - Calendar

Inspirational quotes for each day of the year.

Abundance Zone - Screensaver

Empowering words and pictures, with soothing music.

Abundance Zone - Game

Invaluable for kids of all reading ages.

Teaches vocabulary, spelling, special awareness, positive attitude and sets them up for life.

Abundance Zone - Poster

Great for Kids, for a constant visual reminder of empowering vocabulary.

Abundance Zone - Coaching

Transform your life forever, with personalised and group coaching to master your language and your life.

Visit: **www.TheAbundanceZone.com** or call **+44 (0)20 7379 4383** now for more information on how to best utilise these to help enhance your life.

Recommended Resources

The quality of your life is directly related to the quality of people you spend most of your time with. Therefore it pays to surround yourself with a quality peer group and resources:

Monthly Personal Development Peer Group
The Yes Group is an open vibrant community that inspires people to grow and contribute, and is the leading personal development group in the UK. It holds regular monthly events with top speakers like: Bob Proctor, Brandon Bays, Dan Millman, John Grinder, Keith Cunningham, Mark Victor Hansen, Mike Dooley, Paul Scheele, Peter Thomson, Randy Gage, Robert Young, Topher Morrison and many, many more. www.yesgroup.org

Weekly Personal Development Peer Group
The Leadership Academy Mastermind Group (LAMG) is a London based group of like-minded people interested in personal development, creating an environment that enables each of us to keep focused, keep stepping up, making new distinctions, expanding our identities, becoming all we can in a totally supportive and loving environment whilst playing full out and having abundant fun: www.yahoogroups.com/groups/LAMG

24/7 Online Success Education,
With all-time great speakers like Les Brown, Brian Tracy, Jim Rohn, Dr John Demartini, from the comfort of your home, check out the future of Success Education at Success University: www.TheFuture.SuccessUniversity.com

Coaching and Mentoring
Most abundant and successful people have a coach or mentor, and sometimes they even have several. Whatever area of your life you need help with and want to improve quickly, check out the following:
Coaching: www.MattTraverso.com
Property Coaching: www.Property-Radar.com/Coaching
Youth Coaching: www.YouthCoachingAcademy.com

Masterminding - Peer Group Coaching
Popularised by Napoleon Hill, most successful people have used a form of masterminding on their way to great success. The Masterminding Alliance are leading experts in Masterminding, and are highly recommended: www.TheAbundanceZone.com/Masterminding

Wealth Workout
Everyone needs a regular physical workout to improve their health, and likewise you need a wealth workout to improve your wealth: www.Wealth-Workout.com/TheAbundanceZone

Monthly Success Magazine
Success Formula www.TheAbundanceZone.com/SuccessFormula

Success Events
For a full list of resources & events visit www.TheAbundanceZone.com

Foreword by Robert Dilts to Matt Traverso's book

Coaching for Results

It is a pleasure to write this foreword to Matt Traverso's Coaching for Results. Personal coaching is the process of helping a person to perform at the peak of his or her abilities. It involves drawing out a person's strengths, helping that person to overcome internal resistances and interferences, and facilitating him or her to function as a part of a team.

In this book, Matt Traverso provides readers with the knowledge and tools to accomplish these goals, take charge of their lives and steer themselves toward success. Drawing from his own life experience and his expertise as a coach, mentor and trainer, Matt covers the essential building blocks necessary to build a successful life style: internal state management, using imagination and visualization, setting and achieving goals, using affirmations and incantations, building empowering beliefs and strengthening motivation by clarifying and prioritizing your values.

By integrating principles and know-how form many sources, Matt illustrates how our beliefs and values are the key leverage to creating the life we want. He provides effective and straight forward exercise to help readers identify and transform limiting beliefs as well as define and strengthen empowering beliefs and values.

Matt's writing is clear and easy to read and the book is filled with uplifting quotes and stories, providing a good balance of inspiration and pragmatic tools. Matt's exuberance and enthusiasm for life also comes through in his writing, making it enjoyable to read as well as highly useful. I strongly recommend this book for anyone who wants to improve the quality of his or her life.

Robert Dilts
Famous behavioural scientist and foremost developer of Neuro-Linguistic Programming (NLP).

For more information, visit www.MattTraverso.com

Coaching

As the latest evolution in the personal development industry, coaching helps you to leverage the best of yourself, and attract the success you truly deserve.

How do you currently decide what you do each day? How would that process differ if someone were holding you accountable to achieving the goals you set for yourself and your business?

Your coach will help you set a strategic plan for the future of your business. You will track your progress and your coach will push you. You will develop powerful new habits that are action-oriented.

Do you have an objective sounding board for discussing big decisions?

Your coach's only interest is in helping you succeed. He is not a relative. He is free from all of the limiting beliefs that are holding you back. He exists to help you build the business and the life of your dreams.

Matt Traverso International & The International Professional Coaching Association (IPCA) is a global provider of cutting-edge coaching resources such as live and tele-seminars, one-to-one coaching, conferences, and educational products and services. IPCA provides certified learning programs in the fields of business & executive coaching, coach training and personal transformation for business professionals and the corporate world.

As an agent of change and strategist, Matt is driven by a relentless passion for helping people get what they really want, in business and in life. With more than 10 years' experience as a business coach to people in 11 countries, Matt is an expert at helping clients overcome major obstacles, deal with tough decisions and capitalize on new opportunities to achieve breakthrough results. For more information, visit www.MattTraverso.com ; http://conference.personalcoaching. ws/ipca.htm

The Ultimate NLP Training Manual

The Most Complete Professional Manual for Neuro-Linguistic Programming Practitioner Certification

With a Copyleft Licence

Updated with the most recent NLP developments and techniques

This manual contains the single most practical, readable and innovative treatment of NLP available today. Written by Dr Marco Paret and Matt Traverso in a very easy-to-understand writing style, it covers every key pattern and language-mastery concept in NLP.

Here you will find NLP sequentially presented so that each section builds on the previous one. With a mixture of presentation, example, thought experiments, case studies, outlines, metaphors, etc. the manual trains both conscious and unconscious minds. For master practitioners and trainers, key presentation tools are also included.

This training workbook further includes the latest cutting-edge discoveries about anchoring and the Meta-States Model. No other manual anywhere has all this information with these really new distinctions.

Because it has come out of nine years of actual training sessions of NLP, many of your questions will find answers. All techniques have exercises that follow to lead to behavioural integration of the materials.

For more information visit...

www.nlp4all.biz

Further Recommended Reading

Matt Traverso
Coaching for Results

Matt Traverso & Dr Marco Paret
The Bible of Quantum Coaching
The Ultimate NLP Training Manual

Rhonda Byrne, et al
The Secret

Deepak Chopra
Creating Affluence: The A-Z Guide to a Richer Life

Napoleon Hill
Think and Grow Rich

Anthony Robbins
Awaken The Giant Within

Roger Hamilton
Your Life Your Legacy

T Harv Eker
Secrets of the Millionaire Mind

Bob Proctor
You were Born Rich

Mark Victor Hansen & Robert Allen
The One Minute Millionaire

Mark Victor Hansen & Jack Canfield
Chicken Soup of the Soul series

Brian Tracy
Eat That Frog

Paul R Scheele
PhotoReading

With contributions from well known authors and stars from *The Secret*.

Order your copy of this book now at:

www.prosperity-and-abundance.com

Robert Kiyosaki
Rich Dad, Poor Dad series

Keith Cunningham
Keys to the Vault

Topher Morrison
Settle for Excellence

Kate Ginn
The Secret Learning Code

Mac Attram, Arthur Magoulianiti, Karl Pearsall & Steve Roche
The Power of Masterminding

Caroline Newman, et al
Walking with the Wise - for Overcoming Obstacles

Cathy Breslin and Judy May Murphy
Your Life Only a Gazillion Times Better

David Schwartz
The Magic of Thinking Big

Michael Gerber
The E Myth Revisited

John Gray
Men are from Mars, Women are from Venus

Stephen Covey
First Things First

Stu Mittleman
Slow Burn

For a complete list of recommended reading and to order the above, please visit **www.TheAbundanceZone.com** and get ready to take your life to the next level.

Abundant Events

Transform your Life with Abundance

Can you imagine all the things that you want in your life being there?

What would your life be like if you had an abundance of everything you desired?

Achieving this is in your hands – all you have to do is to take action!

First, you'll need to decide on what actions will put you on the right path – and this is where you'll find lots of opportunities, advice and activities to help you on your way.

Abundant Events was created to help you; your fast track to an abundant life.

We will help you to enjoy an abundant life with:

- Seminars presented by the experts in their fields to expand your knowledge and give you the ideas you need to leverage your lifestyle.

- Workshops to help you to develop and hone new skills that will enable you to move upwards.

- Courses that will educate, enable and entertain – training should be fun!

- Corporate events bringing people together who are like-minded and introducing a range of gurus and high flyers to inspire, motivate and educate.

- Executive and Business coaching – to help individuals to grow, develop and achieve more for themselves and their businesses than they would ever have imagined possible.

Call us on **0845 051 4271** and put yourself on the fast track to an abundant life! Or visit our website

www.AbundantEvents.co.uk

YOUTH COACHING
ACADEMY

A community where we believe

Youth Can

**make a positive difference in their
own lives and those of their peers**

For your <u>free</u> book on
The Essential Youth Coaching Skills
and the opportunities for young people and
those who work with and care for them

please visit

<u>www.youthcoachingacademy.com</u>

Thanks for believing **Youth Can** make a difference

YES Group

The YES Group is an open and vibrant community that inspires people to grow and contribute

"The UK's Leading Personal Development Community"

If you are passionate about personal development and love attending seminars with the worlds most inspiring speakers, yet are prone to lose momentum in between the seminars, then the **YES group** is for you!

We meet on the last Wednesday of every month for an evening of **inspiration**, and **skill development**. We typically feature **dynamic speakers** that will **share** with you the latest and **greatest information** on **personal** and **professional evolution** all for an investment of only **£15**.

Former speakers at YES Group events have included:
Mark Victor Hansen, Dan Millman, Brandon Bays, Bob Proctor, Keith Cunningham, Randy Gage, Paul Scheele, Dave O' Connor, Dr. Topher Morrison, Eric Edmeades, Peter Sage, John Grinder, Mike Dooley, Peter Thomson, Robert Young, Matt Traverso
and many, many more ....

For the latest news on what's happening at the YES Group please visit our website NOW at

www.YesGroup.org.uk

**To check to see if there is a YES Group
in your area of the World please visit**

www.YesGroup.org

If you can't make the events we have amazing interviews with all the speakers and members so there is always an opportunity to capture the wisdom and an opportunity to connect with members.

Steve Oxlade Profile

Steve Oxlade, a new breed of creative Investorpreneur, has been a successful investor since his teens and an Investment Advisor since 1991, and he currently advises clients on property and other investment strategies. Through coaching and mentoring he helps them to identify what strategies are most suitable to enable them to achieve financial success.

His education transitioned from two academic degrees at Durham and Oxford Universities, to real-life practical education and application such as Neuro Linguistic Programming (NLP), Neuro Associative Conditioning (NAC) at Tony Robbins' Mastery University and Leadership Academy, Wealth Strategies at Russ Whitney's Millionaire University, Success University and XL Results Foundation.

An avid traveller and explorer, he has visited over 65 countries and cultures around the world. From his first world trip climbing volcanoes and exploring jungles and ancient civilisation in Java, Borneo and Malaysia, his latest expedition was to the summit of Mount Kilimanjaro, studying wildlife in the Serengeti and Ngorongoro crater and helping to build a school for underprivileged Maasai children.

A keen sportsman since his early school years, where he held numerous school records, he became an accomplished athlete and decathlete in his 20's. He came out of early "retirement" in 2004, to compete at National and International level in X-Training Fitness competitions, and is consistently ranked in the top 5 Masters in the UK. He attributes his exceptional fitness to raw food nutrition, a highly focused mindset, and disciplined preparation and training.

He currently lives in Central London, where he runs the weekly Leadership Academy Mastermind Group (LAMG) which attracts a diverse range of speakers to help members fast-track their way to success.

He is also a strategic adviser to the Yes Group, the UK's leading personal development community, and helps to find world-class speakers for the group's popular monthly events.

His mission is to unleash effortless abundance worldwide, and this book is another massive step towards achieving that dream.

Find out the latest about Steve at: **www.SteveOxlade.com**

Matt Traverso Profile

Matt Traverso is an international business consultant, executive coach and certified trainer of Neuro-Linguistic Programming (NLP). Matt has been training groups, companies, and high-flying business leaders for over 10 years across Europe and around the world. His mission in life is empowering people to create extraordinary lives – helping people make personal breakthroughs that unleash their self expression, personal effectiveness, and leadership.

Through a unique approach combining the latest advancements in human psychology, accelerated learning technologies, and Neuro Linguistic Programming (NLP), Matt delivers innovative, personalized solutions to both individuals and organizations.

One of Europe's most highly-paid coaches, Matt works with entrepreneurs and other business professionals seeking to enhance their business success while deriving a healthy work/life balance that supports their Vision, Mission, and Purpose.

As a trainer and consultant, Matt has empowered and taken the sales forces of multinational corporations to new heights. Companies like, American Express, HSBC, RAS, Monte Dei Paschi, Starwood, L'Oréal, GTS Group are just a few of the companies that have used Matt's insightful and engaging style to train their most valuable asset, their people.

He's worked with speakers like Wayne Dyer, Deepak Chopra, Richard Bandler, Paul McKenna, Robert Dilts, John Grinder, Norman Schwartzkoff, Zig Ziglar, Jim Rohn, and is one of the very few Anthony Robbins Senior Mentors in the world.

A sought after speaker for meetings, conventions, and conferences, he's also a supervisor to a number of training companies for quality control purposes and leads the annual International Coaching Conference in Nice, France. As a professional keynote speaker, Matt delivers compelling speeches on a variety of life-changing subjects such as personal achievement, peak performance, NLP and absolute health.

He's also written two other books – *Coaching for Results* and *The Bible of Quantum Coaching* – and is regularly featured in the press, on radio shows, and on TV. For more information, visit **www.MattTraverso.com**

Please visit

www.TheAbundanceZone.com

to submit any additional inspiring words to go in the next edition, and if we choose your words then your name will be in the book!

Also get your
Free Daily Dose of Abundance

so that you too can now live in...

Printed in the United Kingdom
by Lightning Source UK Ltd.
124712UK00001B/25-156/A